The Sukkah in the Storm

a Sukkot story

The Sukkah in the Storm

a Sukkot story

Rabbi Joseph B. Meszler
Illustrated by Kris Graves

PROSPECTIVE PRESS
Winston-Salem

PROSPECTIVE PRESS LLC
1959 Peace Haven Rd #246, Winston-Salem, NC 27106
www.prospectivepress.com

Published in the United States of America by Prospective Press LLC

TRADEMARK

THE SUKKAH IN THE STORM
Copyright © Joseph B. Meszler, 2022
All rights reserved.
The author's moral rights have been asserted.

Cover and interior art by Kris Graves
© Prospective Press, 2022
The artist's moral right have been asserted.

ISBN 978-1-63516-011-6

ProP-H006

Printed in the United States of America
First Prospective Press softcover printing, August, 2022

The text of this book is typeset in Antiquarian

PUBLISHER'S NOTE:

This story is a work of fiction. The people, names, characters, locations, activities, and events portrayed or implied by this story is the product of the authors imagination or are used fictitiously. Any resemblance to actual people, locations, and events is strictly coincidental. No actual sukkot were harmed in the writing of this book.

Without limiting the rights as reserved in the above copyright, no part of this publication may be reproduced, stored in or introduced into any retrieval system, or transmitted–by any means, in any form, electronic, mechanical, photocopying, recording, or otherwise–without the prior written permission of the publisher. Not only is such reproduction illegal and punishable by law, but it also hurts the author who toiled hard on the creation of this work and the publisher who brought it to the world. In the spirit of fair play, and to honor the labor and creativity of the author, we ask that you purchase only authorized electronic and paper editions of this work and refrain from participating in or encouraging piracy or electronic piracy of copyright-protected materials. Please give authors a break and don't steal this or any other work.

For Barry Fritz

"Weather alert!"
the radio sounded from the window.

Wind swirled.

    Clouds darkened.

        Bright leaves shook and came off the trees.

In a backyard, a little hut, called a sukkah, shivered.

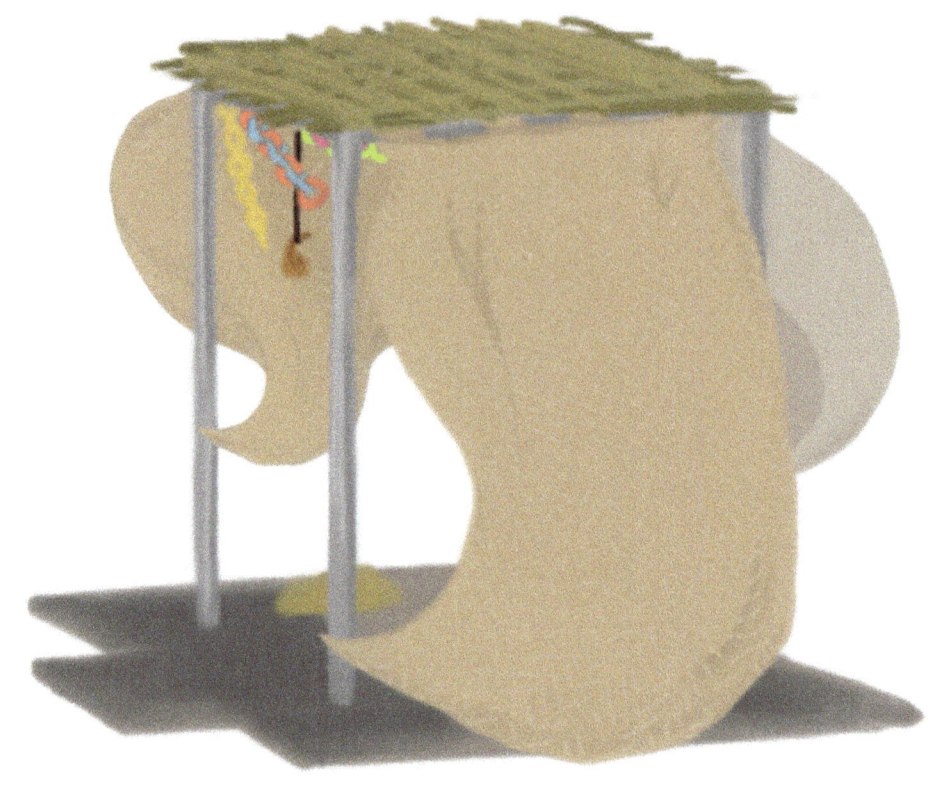

The sukkah had been built for the Jewish holiday called Sukkot.
On this holiday, Jewish people have fun sitting in the sukkah.
They eat and sometimes sleep in it at night.

Sukkot reminds us of long ago when the Israelites traveled through the wilderness. They lived in plain huts. When they set out in the morning, each family took its sukkah apart, and when they stopped, they rebuilt their simple homes.

They did this from campsite to campsite, over and over again.

The sukkah in the backyard was proud of itself. It had a metal frame and three cloth walls tied on with knots. Its roof was made of bamboo, and gourds and paper chains hung from the roof for decoration.

But now a strong wind pushed through the sukkah, making its walls flap and roof tremble.

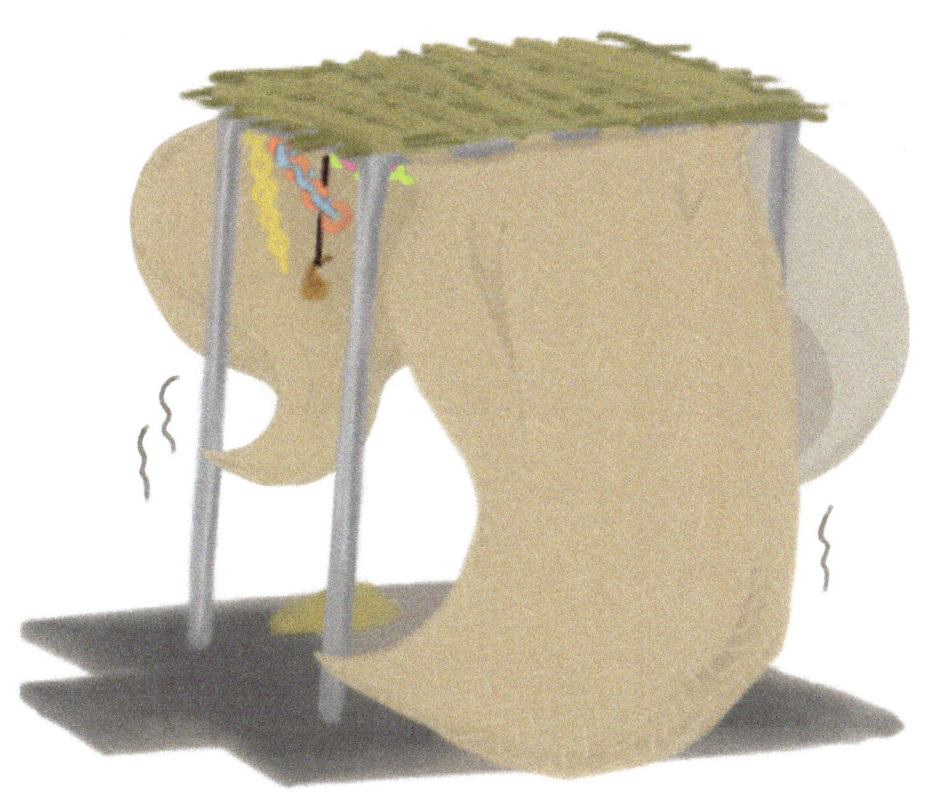

"Weather alert!" the radio barked again. "Hurricane Goliath is going to hit any minute! Take shelter!"

"Take shelter?" the sukkah worried. "I AM shelter! But I am not supposed to be like a real house with bricks or stone. I am only a little hut that reminds people life is fragile. I won't last in a hurricane!"

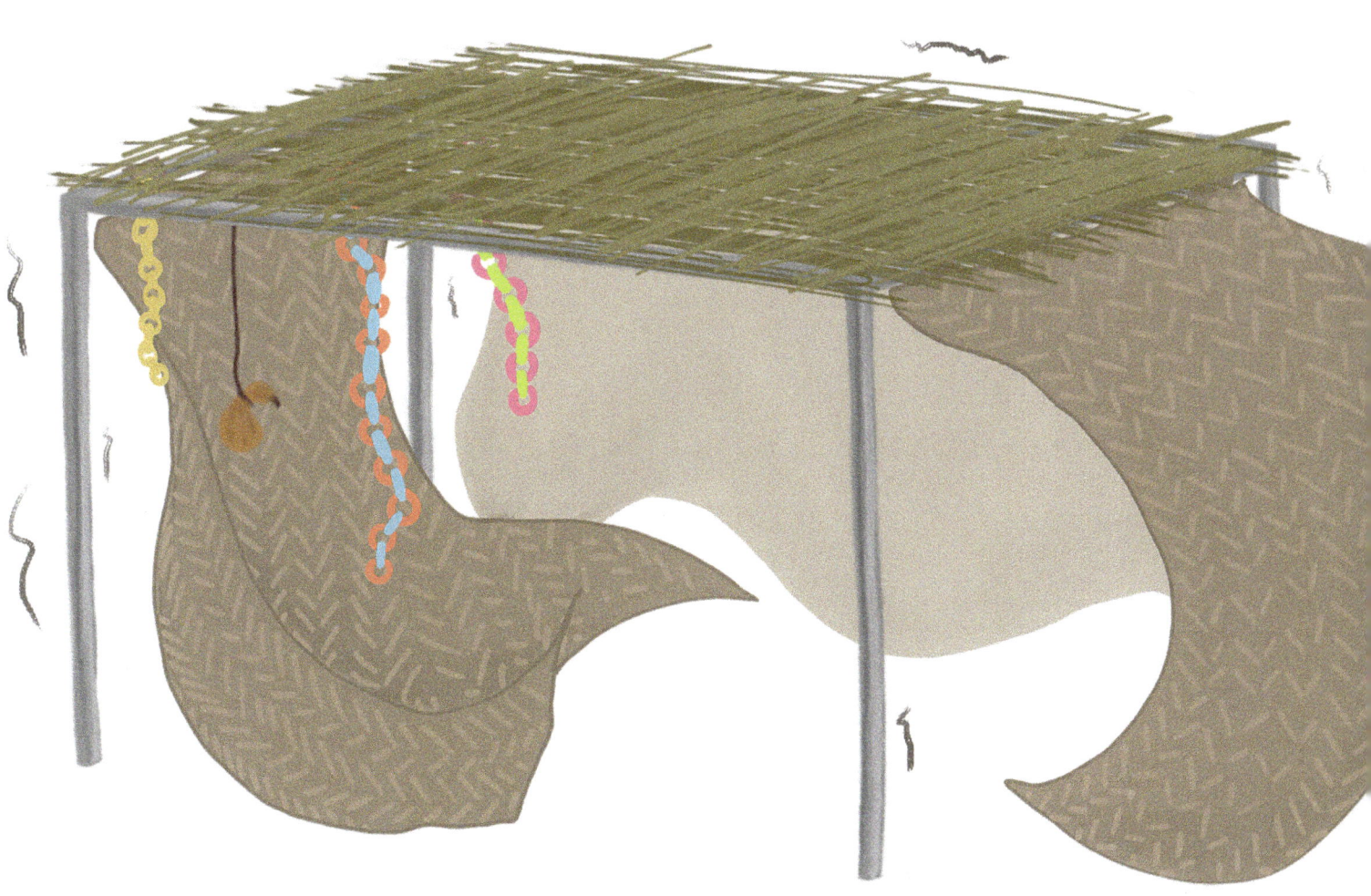

The sukkah tried not to panic.

The wind blew even more fiercely. The sukkah's walls flapped.
The bamboo roof bounced up and down, up and down.
The gourds and paper chains tore off,
some falling to the ground,
some flying away.

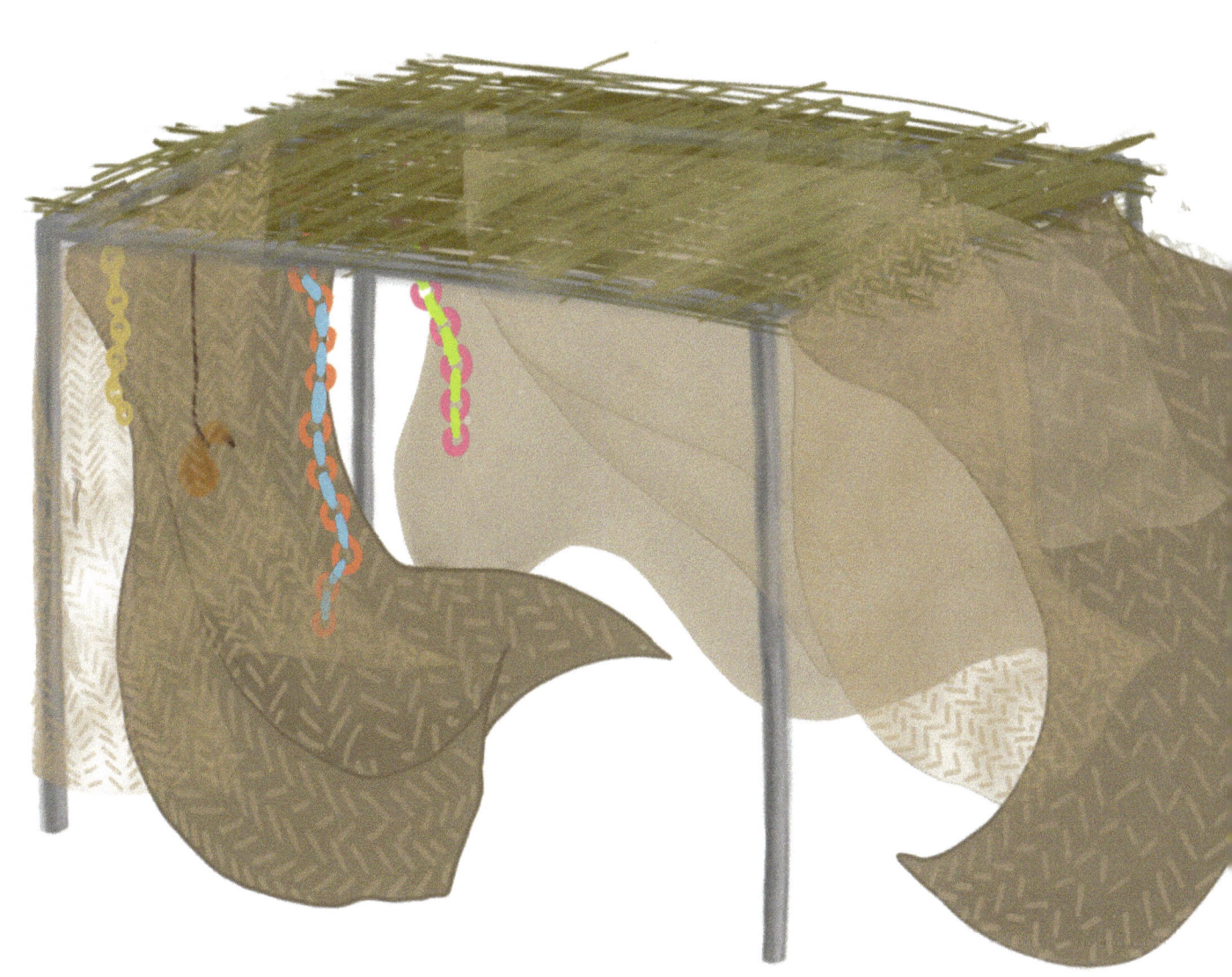

The sukkah stood its ground. It strained to keep itself together even as rain pelted its sides, first this way and then that.

"Everyone, go underground!" the radio called. But the sukkah had nowhere to go. It held on tightly as the hurricane howled through the backyard.

No matter how hard it tried, it was not enough. Off went the roof, straight up into the sky!

The walls flew away!

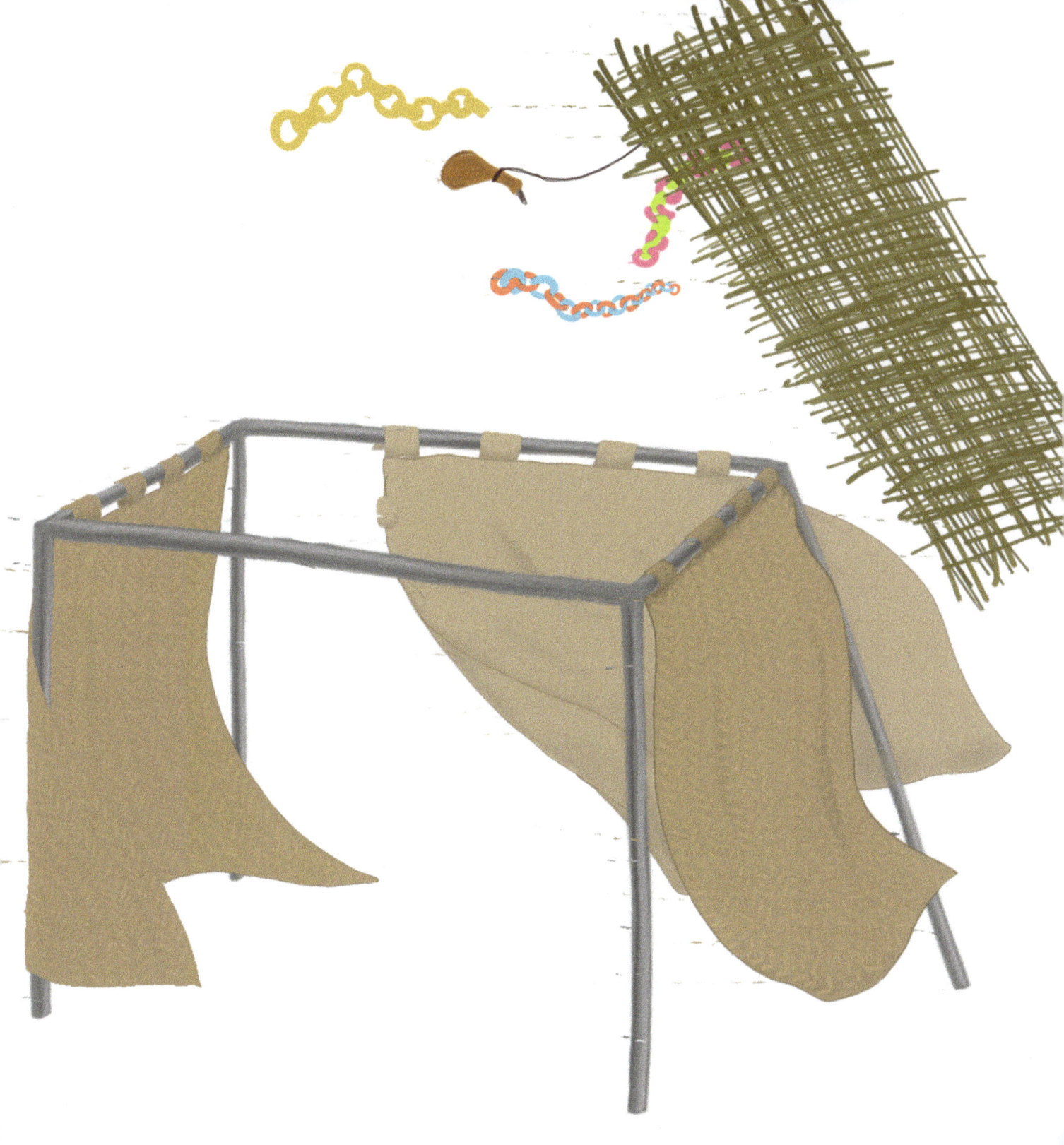

The metal frame rolled over, twisting and banging, crashing and bending until it hit a tree!

The sukkah had fallen apart.

The sky stayed dark for a long time.

Slowly, it grew gray, and then light blue. The rain stopped. The wind became a soft breeze. The sukkah did not know where it was anymore.

It was lost in pieces.

But then hands lifted its frame and put it right-side-up.

Tools clamped and twisted it back into shape.

The cloth walls were found up in the branches of a tree. Fingers gently pulled them down and then stretched and knotted them back into place.

The bamboo roof, which had landed near the street against the mailbox, was carried back with tenderness.

The sukkah felt it tied down anew.

"Not too shabby," the sukkah thought.

"All clear! And the weather looks good for the rest of the week!" the radio announced. "Looks like the coming days will be peaceful."

And what was this?

New gourds and paper chains hung from the roof again, some in shade and some in sun. The sukkah beamed and felt as good as new.

"That's what I do," the sukkah sighed, "just like long ago. I may come apart, but I will always come back together again with hands to help me. I may get knocked down or even scattered, but I will always be rebuilt."

"Over and over again."

Sukkot, otherwise known as the Feast of Tabernacles, is a Jewish holiday that comes after Rosh Hashanah (the Jewish New Year) and Yom Kippur (the Day of Atonement). It is one of the world's earliest holidays of thanksgiving, celebrated for a week during the fall harvest. Jewish people build a hut (a sukkah, plural: sukkot) and leave the security of their homes to eat and possibly sleep outside in the sukkah. During Sukkot, you can see these decorative huts built in yards, on balconies, and even on roofs of tall buildings. At the end of the holiday, the sukkah is disassembled until the next year. The sukkah reminds us of life's fragility, our resilience, and the universal need for shelter and food.

ABOUT THE AUTHOR

Rabbi Joseph B. Meszler is the spiritual leader of Temple Sinai in Sharon, MA, a noted Jewish educator, and a human rights activist. He is the author of several books and many articles, including *The Honey Bee and the Apple Tree* and co-author of *Courageous Candles* with his sister, Joelle M. Reizes (both Prospective Press, 2021).

ABOUT THE ILLUSTRATOR

Kris Graves has been drawing since they were a tiny sprite. After winning a county-wide art competition in the fourth grade, they set their sights on a life of artistry and cats. *The Sukkah in the Storm* is their third illustrated book.

www.ingramcontent.com/pod-product-compliance
Lightning Source LLC
Chambersburg PA
CBHW040613100526
44583CB00041B/3361